MW00474818

Mel Bay's

Classical Repertoire for
RECORDER

By Costel Puscoiu

CONTENTS

FOREWORD

In 1991 I brought out the first edition of my CLASSICAL REPERTOIRE FOR PANPIPES. Now I present CLASSICAL REPERTOIRE FOR RECORDER. This work contains music which I adapted and arranged especially for the recorder. In my opinion classical music is the best basis for learning to play any instrument.

Great performers have proven that the recorder can be succesfully used for playing not only Baroque music, but also symphonic or chamber music from Classical, Romantic or Modern periods just as well as any other musical instrument. No longer is the Romantic or contemporary repertoire considered unfit for the recorder.

Every sincere instrumentalist needs a regular study program. Daily practice of technical exercises and etudes is necessary for improving and maintaining the acquired results. Playing works of music regularly should be the aim of every musician, amateur as well as professional.

It has not been easy to find suitable music for all levels. It was especially diffucult finding simple melodies. I think that, for the beginning player, studying well-known melodies is both easy and enjoyable. I have carefully chosen the best keys for recorder; therefore many songs are not in the keys in which they were originally written. Also a number of other adaptations have been introduced to make the music more suitable for performance on the recorder. The structure of the music has not been altered.

I hope you will find my CLASSICAL REPERTOIRE FOR RECORDER not only instructive and useful, but also pleasant and entertaining. Lots of success.

Delft
December 1994

COSTEL PUSCOIU

ABOUT THE AUTHOR

Costel Puscoiu was born on August 29, 1951, in Bucharest, Romania. He studied and graduated at the "Ciprian Porumbescu" College of Music in Bucharest, majoring in "Composition and Theory." In Romania he worked as a music teacher, and for some years he was a conductor and researcher at the Institute for Ethnology and Folklore in Bucharest. He was also a member of the Society of Romanian Composers.

His compositions comprise symphonic music (symphony, cantatas, concerto for viola), chamber music (string quartets, sonata for clarinet and piano, contemporary for several ensembles, pieces of music for pan flute), choir pieces, and filmscores. His compositions are often influenced by Romanian folklore and Byzantine liturgies. His hand has also appeared in several musicological and folkloristic studies and articles.

In September of 1982 he preferred The Netherlands to his native Romania; now he's working in the music-school department as a pan flute teacher and a leader of an orchestra at "The Free Academy Westvest" in Delft. Meanwhile he has become a member of the Dutch Composers Association.

CHILDREN'S SONG

WOLFGANG AMADEUS MOZART

TO JOY
(from Symphony no.9)

LUDWIG VAN BEETHOVEN

SAINT ANTHONY CHORALE

JOSEPH HAYDN

GAVOTTE

Moderato

MICHAEL PRAETORIUS

FANFARE

Allegro

MICHEL CORRETTE

D.C. al Fine

A I R

Andantino

WOLFGANG AMADEUS MOZART

MINUET

ANONYMOUS

GAVOTTE

GEORG FRIEDRICH HANDEL

OH, TINY CHILD

JOHANN SEBASTIAN BACH

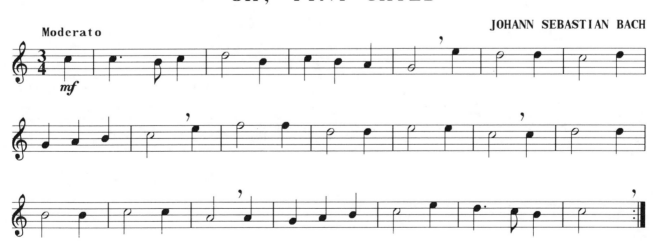

MINUET

JAMES HOOK

ANDANTINO

JEAN-BAPTISTE LULLY

BRUNETTE

JOSEPH BODIN DE BOISMORTIER

MARCH
(from "The Peasants' Cantata")

JOHANN SEBASTIAN BACH

MINUET
(from "Fireworks Music")

GEORG FRIEDRICH HANDEL

MINUET
(from "Fireworks Music")

GEORG FRIEDRICH HANDEL

BRANLE

JOSEPH BODIN DE BOISMORTIER

MELODY
(from "Album for the youth")

ROBERT SCHUMANN

RONDINO

JEAN PHILIPPE RAMEAU

BURLESQUE
(from "Music book for Wolfgang")

LEOPOLD MOZART

SCARBOROUGH FAIR

Andantino grazioso

TRADITIONAL

THE ROYAL MARCH OF THE LION
(from "Le carnaval des animaux")

CAMILLE SAINT-SAENS

Allegro

ANDANTE

JOSEPH HAYDN

Andante

ENGLISH DANCE

HENRY PURCELL

MICHAEL'S SONG

COSTEL PUSCOIU

GAVOTTE

IMPERTINENCE

16

TRUMPET AIR
(from "The Indian queen")

DANIEL PURCELL

GREENSLEEVES

OLD ENGLISH SONG

MINUET

JOHANN KRIEGER

QUADRILLE

JOSEPH HAYDN

BECAUSE WE ARE CHEERFUL

VALENTIN RATHGEBER

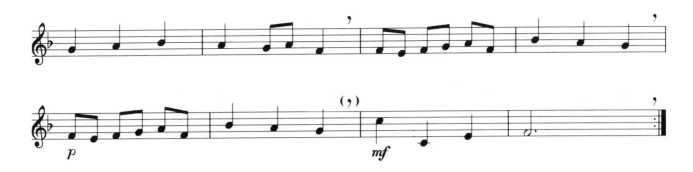

ARIETTA

JOSEPH HAYDN

BOURREE

JOHANN KRIEGER

MINUET

GEORG PHILIPP TELEMANN

RONDEAU

JOSEPH BODIN DE BOISMORTIER

ANDANTE
(from Brandenburg Concerto no.4)

JOHANN SEBASTIAN BACH

PLAISIR D'AMOUR

JEAN PAUL MARTINI

CHORALE
(from "Music book for Anna Magdalena Bach")

JOHANN SEBASTIAN BACH

TAMBOURIN

JEAN PHILIPPE RAMEAU

D.C. al Fine

MARCH
(from "Judas Maccabaeus")

GEORG FRIEDRICH HANDEL

GAVOTTE

ESPRIT-PHILIPPE CHEDEVILLE

LULLABY

JOHANNES BRAHMS

GAVOTTE

Andante

GEORG FRIEDRICH HANDEL

THEME FROM "SWANLAKE"

PIOTR ILICI TCHAIKOVSKY

Moderato
quasi legato

D.C. al Fine

LULLABY

Andante cantabile
quasi legato

WOLFGANG AMADEUS MOZART

GAVOTTE

Allegretto

ARCANGELO CORELLI

WALTZ

JOHANNES BRAHMS

MARTIAL AIR

HENRY PURCELL

MINUET
(from "Music book for Anna Magdalena Bach")

Allegretto

JOHANN SEBASTIAN BACH

SARABANDE

Largo

ARCANGELO CORELLI

A I R

HENRY PURCELL

MARCH
(from the "Occasional Oratorio")

GEORG FRIEDRICH HANDEL

LARGO
(from Opera "Xerxes")

GEORG FRIEDRICH HANDEL

BOURREE
(from Sonata no.2 in G major)

GEORG FRIEDRICH HANDEL

MINUET
(from "Music book for Anna Magdalena Bach")

JOHANN SEBASTIAN BACH

PRELUDIO
(from Sonata in A minor)

ARCANGELO CORELLI

MINUET

Allegretto

GEORG PHILIPP TELEMANN

BERCEUSE

Andantino moderato
quasi legato

GABRIEL FAURE

MUSETTE 1
(from Sonata "La Persane")

PHILBERT DE LAVIGNE

MUSETTE 2

MUSETTE 1 *D.C.*

AVE VERUM

Adagio — quasi legato

WOLFGANG AMADEUS MOZART

ALLEGRO
Allegro moderato   (from Brandenburg Concerto no.5)

JOHANN SEBASTIAN BACH

MINUET

WOLFGANG AMADEUS MOZART

VIVACE
(from Sonata in D major)

JEAN BAPTISTE LOEILLET DE GANT

THE PEACE
(from "Fireworks Music")

GEORG FRIEDRICH HANDEL

ALLEGRO
(from Brandenburg Concerto no.1)

JOHANN SEBASTIAN BACH

TRAUMEREI
(from "Children's scenes" op.15, no.7)

ROBERT SCHUMANN

MINUET

Andante grazioso

WOLFGANG AMADEUS MOZART

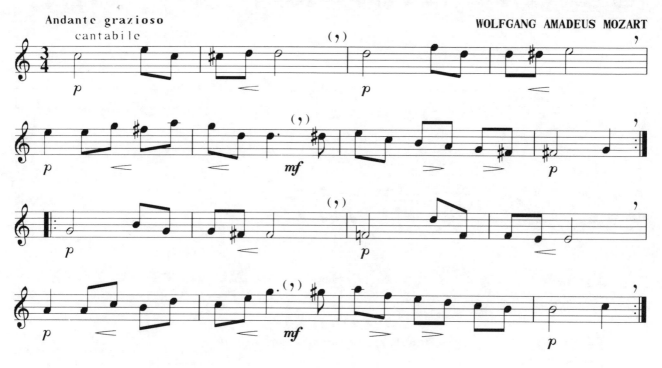

PANIS ANGELICUS

Poco lento

CESAR FRANCK

THEME FROM "AUTUMN"
(from "The four seasons")

ANTONIO VIVALDI

41

MINUET
(from Suite no.2 in B minor)

JOHANN SEBASTIAN BACH

SCHERZO
(from Symphony no.2)

JOHANNES BRAHMS

ETUDE
(op.10, no.3)

FREDERIC CHOPIN

Lento ma non troppo
quasi legato

RONDEAU

ESPRIT PHILIPPE CHEDEVILLE

MARCH OF THE HUNTERS
(from Opera "Der Freischütz")

CARL MARIA VON WEBER

THEME FROM "WINTER"
(from "The four seasons")

ANTONIO VIVALDI

THE DEATH OF ASE

(from "Peer Gynt")

EDVARD GRIEG

ARE YOU WITH ME

JOHANN SEBASTIAN BACH

ADAGIO
(from Sonata in E minor)

Adagio

FRANCESCO GEMINIANI

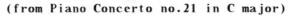

ANDANTE
(from Piano Concerto no.21 in C major)

Andante cantabile

WOLFGANG AMADEUS MOZART

VLAD'S SONG

POLOVETSIAN DANCE
(from opera "Tsar Igor")

Andantino cantabile
con espressione e dolce

ALEXANDER BORODIN

ALLEGRETTO GRAZIOSO
(from Sonata "La Persane")

Gracieusement

PHILBERT DE LAVIGNE

ALLEGRO
(from Sonata in A minor)

DIOGENIO BIGAGLIA

VIVACE
(from Sonata in E minor)

FRANCESCO GEMINIANI

TRUMPET VOLUNTARY

Tempo di marcia
con spirito

HENRY PURCELL
JEREMIAH CLARKE

BOURREE
(from Suite no.2 in B minor)

Allegro

JOHANN SEBASTIAN BACH

ALLEGRO

WOLFGANG AMADEUS MOZART

ALLEMANDA
(from Sonata in A minor)

Allegro moderato

ARCANGELO CORELLI

MOMENT MUSICAL
(Op.94, no.3)

FRANZ SCHUBERT

ALLEGRO GIOCOSO
(from Sonata "La Persane")

Allegro giocoso

PHILBERT DE LAVIGNE

OUVERTURE
(from Suite no.2 in B minor)

Lentement

JOHANN SEBASTIAN BACH

IN THE HALL OF THE MOUNTAIN KING
(from "Peer Gynt")

EDVARD GRIEG

Alla marcia e molto marcato

ALLA HORNPIPE
(from "Water Music")

Allegro vivo

GEORG FRIEDRICH HANDEL

60

D.C. al Fine

SERENADE
(from String Quartet no.17 in F major)

JOSEPH HAYDN

Andante cantabile

AVE MARIA

FRANZ SCHUBERT

RONDEAU
(from Suite no.2 in B minor)

JOHANN SEBASTIAN BACH

MINUET IN G

REJOICING
(from "Fireworks Music")

GEORG FRIEDRICH HANDEL

POLONAISE
(from Suite no.2 in B minor)

JOHANN SEBASTIAN BACH

SINFONIA
(from Cantata no.156)

JOHANN SEBASTIAN BACH

SLAVONIC DANCE
(Op.46, no.4)

ANTONIN DVORAK

SOLVEJG'S SONG
(from "Peer Gynt")

EDVARD GRIEG

PAVANE

Allegretto molto moderato

GABRIEL FAURE

ALLEGRETTO
(from Symphony no.3)

JOHANNES BRAHMS

ROMANCE
(from "Eine kleine Nachtmusik")

WOLFGANG AMADEUS MOZART

AIR
(from Suite no.3 in D major)

JOHANN SEBASTIAN BACH

ALLEGRO
(from Sonata "La Persane")

PHILBERT DE LAVIGNE

Leggiero e marcato

GIGUE

ARCANGELO CORELLI

AVE MARIA

JOHANN SEBASTIAN BACH
CHARLES FRANCOIS GOUNOD

Andante religioso

MINUET

Allegro moderato

LUIGI BOCCHERINI

TRIO

D.C. al Fine

WALTZ
(from Opera "Tsar Igor")

ALEXANDER BORODIN

JESU, JOY OF MAN'S DESIRING
(from Cantata no.147)

JOHANN SEBASTIAN BACH

ALLEGRO
(from Brandenburg Concerto no.3)

JOHANN SEBASTIAN BACH

Allegro moderato

staccato

mf (*f*)

THE SWAN
(from "Le carnaval des animaux")

MINUET
(from "Eine kleine Nachtmusik")

WOLFGANG AMADEUS MOZART

SONG WITHOUT WORDS
(Op.62, no.6)

FELIX MENDELSSOHN-BARTHOLDY

Allegretto grazioso

SERENADE

FRANZ SCHUBERT

PROMENADE
(from "Pictures at an exhibition")

Allegro giusto nel modo russico;
senza allegreza, ma poco sostenuto

MODEST MUSSORGSKY

THE OLD CASTLE
(from "Pictures at an exhibition")

Andante molto cantabile e con dolore
con espressione (legato)

MODEST MUSSORGSKY

THE GREAT GATE OF KIEV

(from "Pictures at an exhibition")

Allegro alla breve
Maestoso. Con grandezza

MODEST MUSSORGSKY

INTRODUCTION
(from Oboe Concerto)

DOMENICO CIMAROSA

THE ELEPHANT
(from "Le carnaval des animaux")

CAMILLE SAINT-SAENS

HUMORESQUE
(Op.101, no.7)

ANTONIN DVORAK

DOUBLE
(from Suite no.2 in B minor)

JOHANN SEBASTIAN BACH

BADINERIE
(from Suite no.2 in B minor)

Allegro giocoso

JOHANN SEBASTIAN BACH